C000092836

EDUCATION 2020:
Time to abandon Bloom's Taxonomy

Kathiravelu Ganeshan

@Ganeshan

Preface

Blooms Taxonomy has been used extensively by people in the education sector for more than sixty years. Millions, perhaps billions, of person-hours have been spent studying Bloom's taxonomy and applying it in education. Bloom's taxonomy has been used one way, or another, to produce tens, may be hundreds, of thousands of research papers and tens of thousands of master and doctorate theses.

In this minimalist book, I argue that Bloom's taxonomy did not help advance facilitation of learning or help make learning an enjoyable activity. For the most part, it served as a tool to justify continuing the nineteenth century model of teaching, hindering the adoption of alternative and much better ways of facilitating learning.

Bloom's taxonomy is certainly neither relevant, nor useful, in the current era. It is high time that we abandoned it for the benefit of future generations.

Do we need a Taxonomy in Education?

Some infants (children less than one year old) are able to use a tablet PC or a mobile phone better than some adults. They may not be able to use all the functionalities of these devices. But, then how many adults are capable of using all the functionalities of these devices, even after receiving training from experts? Taking it one more step, how many of these experts know how to use all the functionalities?

Many toddlers create art, music and other artefacts on these devices. These toddlers learn; *remember, understand, apply, analyse, evaluate* and *create*. And they do this at a level that some adults with a bachelor, master or doctorate qualification cannot match, in specific areas.

Isn't it time we free up education from the thinking that schools and universities need to have *levels* like Year 1 and 2, and *courses* like Economics 101 and Music 304?

What I am suggesting is that we should stop breaking down and siloing the process of learning and achievement into things like *remember, understand, apply, analyse, evaluate* and *create.*

Many young people are creating games and other artefacts. For example, two school children in New Zealand devised a system for tracking rip currents in the sea, and warn swimmers. It was a complex project and they used every one of the six levels; *remember, understand, apply, analyse, evaluate* and *create.* Are we going to give them a doctorate, master or a bachelor degree?

On the other hand, how many people with an undergraduate or postgraduate qualification cannot think beyond what their professors taught them?

The mental processes associated with learning are complex and interrelated. Breaking these up and siloing these into artificial entities does not help advance the facilitation of learning.

Trying to classify these complex and interrelated mental processes is, in my view, a waste of time. It also distracts us from more useful pursuits.

Using any such classification in education, especially in the era of the Internet, YouTube, Wikipedia, smart machines, self-driving cars, pilotless aircraft, and machine learning, is in my view, a disservice to future generations.

If some people need research topics so they can get a master or doctorate qualification in education, I suggest that they look elsewhere, instead of trying to break these complex, interrelated mental processes and siloing these, and using these to create barriers to actual learning.

Static devices like microchips, and mobile devices like robots, drones and self-driving cars, and other autonomous vehicles are being programmed to learn; *remember, understand, apply, analyse, evaluate* and *create.*

Are we going to apply Bloom's taxonomy to these machines? Or, waste our time coming up with a modified Bloom's taxonomy, or a new taxonomy? What is the purpose? How will any such activity help solve any of the major problems facing humanity?

I am also suggesting that the knowledge, skills and other relevant attributes of an individual should take precedence over qualifications. Businesses are gradually beginning to recognise this and changing the way they make decisions when hiring new employees.

In the following chapters, I look at some interesting examples that will help further my case.

Amira Willighagen

Amira Willighagen, was just nine years old when she won the sixth season of Holland's Got Talent in 2013.

https://www.youtube.com/watch?v=qDqTBl KU4CE

When asked by one of the judges, if she had a singing teacher, Amira answered in the negative. Compare Amira with the millions of children whose parents spend a fortune and a significant portion of their lives driving Mum's or Dad's taxis, ferrying these children to and from music classes, week-after-week, for several years, often, with not much to show for their efforts.

Did Bloom's taxonomy help in any way?

Lydian Nadhaswaram

In 2019, Lydian Nadhaswaram, a twelve year old from Chennai, India, won *The World's Best* competition, against all odds, beating formidable competition that included large groups of adults from around the world.

Lydian Nadhaswaram thrilled the audience, the judges and the other competitors with some amazing feats, including playing a piano at 325 beats, playing Mozart blindfolded and, playing two separate pieces with two different time signatures, simultaneously on two pianos.

Seeing the amazing knowledge and skills of Lydian and another young contender (Daneliya Tuleshova), Dimash Kudaibergen, an older contender whom many expected to win the competition, withdrew from the competition, wanting to let the younger

Lydian or Daneliya have a better chance of winning the first ever *The World's Best* title and one million dollars.

During a follow up interview, Lydian's father told the interviewer that he did not send Lydian, or his sister, to regular school, choosing instead to home school them.

How did Bloom's taxonomy help Lydian on his journey?

There are, of course, so many such stories, throughout history, from all around the world in the field of music. In the next couple of sections, we will look at some examples in sports.

Swimming Coaches

Over the past eleven years, I have observed at least fifty swimming coaches teaching students injury-inducing and unnecessary techniques like twisting the forearm so the thumb enters the water first, and getting their students to use the standard drill of leg kicking while holding a kickboard with both arms, with the head held above the water. I never dared even to broach the topic with any of these coaches as they are the instructors, and these are drills and techniques that have been is use for decades. An adult who learnt the *importance* of thumb-first entry from one of these coaches even tried to help me *correct* my technique.

Indeed, a little bit of research will show that there are better ways of teaching swimming.

Any way we can apply Bloom's taxonomy here?

"Double-handed" Tennis Champions

A handful of top tennis players hold the racket with both hands for both forehand and backhand strokes. They go against the norm. Most of them likely would have had to suffer some stress and stand their ground to fight off the advice given by some of their coaches at some stage.

Could Bloom's taxonomy have made it easier for these players to resist the pressure from the coaches?

Front Crawl Swimming

The front crawl style of swimming (which is often referred to as freestyle, as the front crawl is the fastest style of swimming and therefore used by all swimmers in freestyle races) was introduced to Europe not that long ago. There are a couple of versions of when and how the front crawl arrived in Europe; one version mentions Europeans discovering the front crawl when they saw some South Americans using the front crawl in some competition in the UK; and the other version, an Australian learning it from a Solomon Islander. Let us imagine, for a moment, what swimming coaches in Europe may have been teaching prior to the arrival of the front crawl.

Any help from Bloom's taxonomy in bringing the front crawl to Europe?

Teaching Only What One Knows

Indeed, in almost any discipline, we can find several examples of established schools and coaches stuck with teaching what they know and not questioning and exploring if there are better ways of doing things.

Has this been the same with Bloom's taxonomy over the past sixty plus years?

Economic Theories

The economic theories that were developed over the last several decades are not serving us well anymore, extending the gap between the rich and the poor.

What is being taught as economics in schools and universities? Why has this not changed yet to at least begin addressing the problems facing humanity?

Can Bloom's taxonomy help?

Living in Bubbles

For many years, the rest of the world did not know anything about surfing or stand-up-paddle-boarding even though the Polynesians had been surfing and stand-up-paddle-boarding for a long time.

The rest of the world had no idea of the front crawl style of swimming until they saw someone from the Solomon Islands or South America do it.

In some cases, pockets of knowledge evolved independently at two, or more, separate parts of the world. For example, coracles, called *parisals* in Tamil Nadu, South India seem to have been in use in several parts of the world, including South India, and Wales, for millennia.

The Tamils also made rafts by tying together a few square-shaped logs cut from tree trunks and called these *kattumaram*.

The Tamil word *kattumaram* is the origin of the English word catamaran. Catamarans are now a popular form of stable boats with two or more hulls.

Sri Lankan and South Indian fishermen also used the *kattumaram* as a sort of a stand-up-paddle-board in deep water and, like a punt (as in punting in Oxford), in shallow water using long bamboo poles for propulsion. I speak from experience as I have done some punting in Oxford and, also had a lot of fun using a *kattumaram* in Sri Lanka.

The catamarans used in the America's Cup races *fly* over water, with the hydrofoils lifting them well above the surface.

Stand-up-paddle-boarders have recently started using foils as well.

Did Bloom's taxonomy help in any way?

Education

According to the Cambridge Dictionary, education is *"the process of teaching or learning, especially in a school or college, or the knowledge that you get from this"*. https://dictionary.cambridge.org/dictionary/english/education Retrieved 31 August 2019.

Right below this definition, the dictionary provides the following as the first example of the use of the word, education, in a sentence: *"As a child he **received** most of his education at home."*

The Oxford Dictionary defines education as *"a process of teaching, training, and learning, especially in schools or colleges, to improve knowledge and develop skills"*.

Learning can happen without teaching. When a child observes an adult doing something and copies it, the adult is not teaching, but the child learns. When a child comes into physical contact with an open flame, the child learns; the flame is not teaching the child. Learning can and does happen anywhere and at any time.

Over the past couple of millennia, we have evolved our education system, bundling learning with teaching and linking this tightly-coupled teaching/learning process to schools and colleges and even making schooling compulsory for all children, and employers asking for certificates, diplomas and degrees awarded by schools and colleges as evidence of one's knowledge or abilities.

When humans lived in isolated societies, with no internet, Wikipedia or YouTube, it took a long time for knowledge to spread.

A student of music, during the time of Mozart, for example, certainly needed a teacher. If Amira or Lydian were born in that era who knows how things would have turned out for them, or how they may have changed music?

If someone wanted to learn school math or physics or chemistry in the 1960s, they could learn most of the theory from books, without a teacher and only needed access to the lab equipment, chemicals and the instruction sheets to do the practical work; I know, because that is exactly what I did, and I know several others who did. Remember, there was no internet and no simulated experiments in any subject; just paper books and physical laboratory equipment and actual chemical compounds.

Today, many large lecture halls in universities often have just a few students attending the lectures; the lecturers record their lectures and make these available online; the students either attend the lecture via video links or review the material later, asynchronously. Do we need these large lecture halls? Can we avoid the time and fuel wasted by students and lecturers commuting to give or attend these lectures?

How many of these lectures are updated from one semester to the next? When it comes to basic subjects like Economics 101 or Physics 101 in a university, or statistics or history in a school, what changes from one year to the next? Do the Laws of Supply and Demand or Newton's Laws of Motion change from one term to the next?

In any case, who assures that the material delivered by the "teacher" meets the learning outcomes, is at the right level, correct and relevant? How do we know that the lecturer has given a good lecture?

Here come the teaching and learning experts and the compliance police, often armed with Bloom's taxonomies!

Exploiting Bloom's Taxonomy

In the three countries where I spent most of my teaching career, every lecturer/professor was expected and, more often than not, required, to attend classes and workshops conducted by *Teaching and Learning Experts* who *help* the teachers improve their teaching.

During these classes and workshops, more often than not, the attendees, all academics, would sit bored and complaining; seldom, did we have an engaging class or workshop.

In many instances, the academics were told that they must attend, and attendance was taken and those who did not attend, reported to management.

If these *Teaching and Learning Experts* added any real value, wouldn't most academics attend these classes and workshops willingly?

Indeed, every now and then we had someone who helped us improve our teaching, but in most cases it was a waste of time.

In one case, it was even decreed that ALL staff must attend a long series of sessions conducted by these *Teaching and Learning Experts*, collect evidence in the form of photographs, blogs and other paraphernalia and submit this evidence to obtain a Practice Passport.

Those who did not complete this exercise and obtained a Practice Passport would no longer be able to teach in that institution, including the ones who had achieved great results and were recognised by students as the best teachers in the institution, year after year.

Such ill-conceived ideas that almost always came from people, who had not taught a class in years, but somehow found their way into management not only wasted a lot of time and resources but also frustrated the educators who wanted to get on with the job of helping students learn.

Indeed there are a few really great, *true learning and teaching experts* who have helped, and continue to help teachers and lecturers, especially those in the early stages of their careers. Usually these *true learning and teaching experts* play a mentoring role and seldom come up with new forms, policies, rules or *compulsory* workshops. They engage in fruitful conversations with those at the coalface of education.

Please email me your experiences and I will collate all responses, without divulging your identities and post a graph on Twitter, LinkedIn and any other platform that readers may suggest.

ganeshan8@hotmail.com

Compliance Police

Great educators continue to leave the sector for good, frustrated by the policies and practices developed by these *teaching and learning experts* and the demands of the *compliance police*. Many others stay around and do their best within the constraints imposed by these policies and practices.

What is more important, (and I believe at least 90% of all teachers and academics in some countries will agree) is that compliance costs too much time, has significant negative impact on creativity and student learning and experience and that teachers and institutions often find ways of meeting the requirements, by cheating.

People who enjoy learning and helping others learn continue to learn and help others learn.

In my view, it is often those who do not enjoy being part of the community of learners who work their way through the system and become *experts* and *compliance police*.

Bloom's taxonomy is often used by the teaching and learning experts and compliance police to justify their existence.

A Different Perspective: K-12 Education in the US vs China and other countries

Keith Ballard, *2003 Milken U.S. Educator* had been studying Education since the early 2000s and has, on YouTube, a few videos of his interviews with various TV channels. He argues passionately about the need for improving K-12 education in the US. He claims that if the problems are not fixed, the US is going to be "looking at something equivalent the modern fall of Rome." https://www.youtube.com/watch?v=QJPzy4JfknQ

I am wondering if Bloom's taxonomy caused this problem too.

Questions

If the understanding and application of Bloom's taxonomy made any difference to education, why do we continue to have a sizeable proportion of students failing courses and programs?

Why do we have so many students dropping out of university, especially at postgraduate level?

Why do students resort to plagiarism and other forms of cheating?

Are some of the certificates, diplomas and degrees including postgraduate degrees worth the paper they are written on?

Does one need a paper qualification to succeed in the real world? To make a positive contribution to the real world?

Are there better ways of working with learners and prepare ourselves better to meet the challenges we all face as the human race?

About the Author

Kathiravelu Ganeshan has extensive experience teaching at universities, polytechnics and private colleges in Australia, New Zealand, Singapore, Sri Lanka, and the USA. He has more than sixty publications, including eight books. He enjoys learning and helping others become life-long learners. Ganeshan loves swimming and catching waves on a SUP. *"Learning should be fun, not a chore."*